where once

Poems by

Sally Allen McNall

MAIN STREET RAG PUBLISHING COMPANY
CHARLOTTE, NORTH CAROLINA

Cover art: "Six Wooden Blocks," G. Daniel Massad
Author photo by: Scott McNall

Acknowledgments:

Café Review, "Goodbye to Byzantium."
Nimrod, "world cup," "What is beneath our feet"
Tertulia Magazine, "Interpretation"
The Wild Goose Review, "Seize the day"
Left Curve, "What has Athens to do with Jerusalem"
Arsenic Lobster, "Six Wooden Blocks"
The Chariton Review, "Love and Beauty"
Tertulia Magazine, "Interpretation"
The Comstock Review, "The Iron thing they carried"
Persimmon Tree, "Escape from the Hospital,"
Umbrella Journal, "Cease your struggle"
Right Hand Pointing, "All day in the open"
The MacGuffin, "Fallings from us, vanishings"
Wilderness House: "River, mountain," "Shelter,"
    "Extending a metaphor"
Barrow Street, "Make your answer"
Poetry East, "Lens"
The Write Room, "Drought," "In Scar," "Invoking Whitman"

The following poems also appeared in the chapbook, *Trying to Write a Poem without the Word Blood in It,* (PWJ Publishing, **YEAR**): "Make your answer," "Interpretation," "Concrete Particulars," "Going to the theatre"

Library of Congress Control Number: 2010933618

ISBN: 978-1-59948-263-7

Produced in the United States of America

Main Street Rag
PO Box 690100
Charlotte, NC 28227
www.MainStreetRag.com

to Scott

CONTENTS

Time Spent Waiting

Nothing Lost

Sally Allen McNall

Envoi

Make your answer a story

Give me the particulars, I say, bone,
blood meeting the air. Describe
famished flesh eating itself
I say, and the odorless colorless
poison entering one cell
on the surface of the tongue,
one mouth, how it is sped
outward by contact, rumor,
in the air, and in a form of words
hastily assembled long ago
for a different purpose,
now lively venom, vaccine
against hope. Tell me how you live,
I say. What act, what room
in your days do you call
ease? What is pleasure?
How is each transmitted?
You must indicate
the worth, the consequences
of what delicacy you have taken for yourself,
how the quiet was paid for
and who helped you.
Make your answer a story,
make the people in the story endlessly
recognizable, loveable even, make them long for peace,
make their bones tremble where they are hiding,
make their blood full of longing. Begin.

Goodbye to Byzantium

Goodbye to Byzantium

> *This is our body.*
> —Gary Snyder

Blue-white sphere spun in dark: home, its inviolable laws.
Wrenched alignment, just more hammered stardust.
The two inseparable. Bruised to pleasure.

Pain in hidden emplacements firing on innocents,
a cramp or no, a stab. Is it tender
here, along new border, desert, coastline?

It is tender where I cannot go.
Baghdad, where once gardens.
A shore where once wild strawberries this small.
Beirut, Ramallah: "We love whatever we can."
The blackened vine. Sometimes as if a sudden blow,
or, just there, a burning will begin.

After thirty years, she went back to Tehran.
Veiled, came back with veils. We all tried to put on
knowledge. An ache. More than touch it. Wear it—

Stretch this shrinking cabin of green wood.
Loosen the heart's jesses. Poets torque toward shy engineers
and scientists—together we have this handful of decades.
Turning. Cursing monotonously. Crying.
Widening toward.

2006

Every fruitless flower

Again it's April. The dogwoods, with their petals that
bear the stigmata, are in full flower—white, rose, and the color
of blood in water—floating out on their black branches.
They're not native to this plundered coast, nor am I,
yet I love as well the small bell flower of the native manzanita,
which burns so hot and white it is sacred to the first
people here. For seven months now I've tried to think past
these fictions: the state, borders, enemies. I have to admit
it's not working. My Bosnian friend sends an e-mail
petition, to charge Ariel Sharon with war crimes. Because
I'm going next month to the Middle East, I've bought scarves,
so I can cover. Good idea, she tells me.

That afternoon a young man, his checkered *intifada* scarf
around his shoulders, hands me a leaflet about a vigil.
I can't, I say to him, giving all my heart to our civility,
I promised this evening to my mother. It's the right
excuse, though I want immediately to stop, ask him about his
mother, and cannot.

Native azalea, and the golden foreign kind.
Lilac, locust blossom. I think of Dijana's crescent
moon and five-pointed star, always against her skin.
It's a cultural thing, she says. I could buy a cross, that
would be a cultural thing, and then no one would mistake me
for a Jew. I consider this, for days.

I tell my Jewish friends, and the anthropologist says
*it's best not to wear any religious symbol, not to attract
any attention.* So though I linger at jeweler's windows

                                                    Sally Allen McNall

for another week, I don't buy a cross, though I want,
miserably, to take her dare.

The orange poppy, the dark red iris, the way the oak leaves
green, against this deep western sky. Either the dark red iris
matters, or nothing does. The trucks idle at the periphery
of the refugee camp. A young woman detonates explosives strapped
to her body. I want, miserably, every useless flower and leaf in the world
to protest, to curl back into bud and bulb, so all
of us would miss them.

April, 2002

world cup

When Senegal won its World Cup match
with France, four young men in the hotel lobby
in Istanbul shouted in joy, and I—
tourist, American, old lady—yelled
"Down with the colonial powers!"
And every one of the men, and my husband,
laughed. A good moment, a little
surprise, maybe, for some of our allies fallen
on hard times. As haven't they all.

There is no place in the world I can go now
and check this bitterness,
set it down and leave it to pick up later.

I have fallen in love, as they say, four times
with four foreign capitals. I did not at eighteen
understand why Vienna was sad. Much later
I saw Beijing, and then Petersburg.
By then I understood, why a place of extravagance
and settled grief enters me like a lost love.

People will travel for days to stand and brood
over a battlefield, trying to remember
what they have never seen, and perhaps
say a prayer.

In Istanbul there are too many palaces, and
too many hotels. In the outlying districts,
too many "midnight" houses, run up illegally
in the dark. Too many carpets,
ornamental tiles, young men with time
on their hands, too many wedding dresses of every
description, lira to the dollar, corrupt—
or so the guide told us—politicians. Far too many
old stories, glasses of tea, young men in the military,

                                          Sally Allen McNall

heartstopping gardens and vistas of hill, mosque, minaret,
slow blue water, and gray and gold cloud.

By the time Turkey lost its match to Brazil, I wanted
never to leave, I wanted to suffer the excess
for another thousand years.

October 2002

What is beneath our feet

for Dijana and Marina

1. Half way round the world

We come out of our small hotel with the muzzeins' mid-morning call.
Step this way, sir, lady, say the carpet barkers, *come in, come in and see.*
We go in, accept the glass of tea, count knots, go barefoot on the pile,
fooling no one, ask for a wet white rag to test the dyes.

2. Two summers

In the last summer of the sixties, both the little girl
in Bosnia and the American girl in Greece
were always heading for shade or water—
the plane tree, the arbor, high wall,
the Aegean sea and the Adriatic sea,
and in Mostar, the Neretva river
beneath the old single arch bridge.

        Day after day in Greece cast in bronze,
        molten, emblems struck forever
        in the mind's eye. Black billy goats
        fighting on the beach at Marathonos.
        A boy seated in the middle branches
        of a fig tree, sweetness let go again and again
        from his opened hand to children below.
        Two women scrubbing a faded carpet
        on the cement beside a water trough.
        The first sight of the long-abandoned abbey Belle Pais
        at the last turn of the climb, doors open
        north and south on white air, blue ocean.

                                        Sally Allen McNall

While the American girl left Greece, drove up
the coastline—Dubrovnic, Split— the little girl
in nearby Mostar ran with others from house
to house, washing carpets. In courtyards
on mosaics of worn stone they worked
the soap in, with torn up potato-bag burlap,
and they turned the hoses on each other,
on the brilliant and complex patterns,
they rolled the carpets up over the family's towels,
bit by bit, perching and bouncing on the roll
like rows of trilling big-eyed birds.

3. *Real Estate Services in the Displaced Greek Communities of*
Turkish-Occupied Cyprus

California coastal weather, gray sky,
light fog—foils for these layered autumn leaves.
The flaring trees reveal, conceal themselves
where I walk. I think of another morning
like this—hushed, a little away
from the world:
In the spring of 1969, we went
to Cyprus, to Lefkosia, to Ömeriye
mosque. In those days, the faithful
left their prayer rugs in place, in layers.
We went barefoot. So many.
So different, each from each.

On my computer screen, the Greek Cypriot girl
traces the line between the two parts
of her country, points out ghost villages.
The invasion was in seventy-four.
My whole family fled Morfou,
leaving everything. It wasn't much, they had
no carpets, they had no floors.

And later, *Of course some*
of the Turkish Cypriots thought
they were being saved. And then,
Some were. We talk about the UN.
Cynic: a Greek
word for us both.

This morning I try again to take in the peace
of the unmoving trees.
I have purposely left out the floors
of the great mosques of Istanbul,
the same pattern repeated now on carpet wall
to wall. I have left out my carpets.
I have left out the Greek orchards
the Turkish rescuers razed.

November 2002

Sally Allen McNall

Drought

Where the March rains fail the hand-tilled fields again
And fewer fishing boats with crimson nets put out each year
Where the Sahara shifts north and west, not slowly

Where rivers speak to the people in familiar voices
And the soil still speaks, the clouds, the burden of sun
Where the people have known for years what is happening

Where at all seasons the nomads arrive from the mountains
and every city wears its poor like a broken halo
Where the skills of millennia are not taught to the children

Where the heart of each desert city is still walled and beating
nothing is wasted, nothing is easy or obvious
I can see only the surface, the blank face of the future

July 2009

Month, year

Now, to feel safe, I set down poems in their
months, years. Before. After. During.

Words I keep by me: blood, dust, water, tree, hope, waste, life.
A friend visits Tel Aviv, says no one now picks up the trash.

Outside Dresden, miles of empty Soviet apartments, like Detroit,
missing windows, old fires, sprayed tags, up to the second floor.

My husband, son, grandson visit the ancestral Pueblos in their caves.
I visit prehistory in Niedersachsen, and think

of cairns in the Highlands, stones upon stones, tombs,
and the forts, the tiny monasteries in Ireland. The short lives

of people six thousand, even one thousand years ago—tomb builders,
working out the idea of human time, keeping it safe,

knowing what they could, of what might come.

August 2009

                                                    Sally Allen McNall

Hard Places

Persia

The spirit world is so enormous
It presses all around us
his hands draw it in from the whole room
from the night outside
It will have its way with us
his hands fall open, abject

I answer *as when in the desert*
we are overtaken
by a sandstorm
and turned toward another path

We have done it this way
for a thousand years

at sunset
on the edge of Fes
the open orange fire breathed out hard
stoked by fat olive pits
beside a hack-marked hill
of hard blue clay

a dozen youngsters
slowed and kicked their potter's wheels
shaped
held thin brushes steady
as pots went round
I held back to see it   no image familiar
only the essential star
or palm   lotus   red   or indigo

In my country   too   first people
drew like this for ten thousand years
the essential bird   squash blossom   cloud
even the hand shaped cartoons were

the human hand

a girl takes a saffron tile
sets free with her slim chisel
a small shape like a Z
then another just like it
to be set fast in some mosaic

                                        Sally Allen McNall

one at a time   ceiling or floor

the foreman sees
when the tile cracks

he is quick and picks up
from the floor the unfinished
example

For you, madam, yes, free, free.
Original!

with it in my pocket I go out
into the now fallen dark

February 2009

Hard places

On these rich farmlands by the Mediterranean,
he said, *we grow the fruit and vegetables for industrial Europe*

later, in the south, we saw nomads
follow their flocks

on the dry hills where the wildest honey grows

adobe, pisé, rammed earth, dirt
houses that melt in rain

(two towers that melt in fire

supply chains losing links one at a time
then in increasing number)

wherever you go in the world someone says don't encourage the beggars

so many

I say on the phone I have given alms to Muslims and my friend
says *shut up shut up* hangs up
                e-mails me *you could be accused*
                of giving money to terrorists

You can't live the Berber's life,
he said, *without some hard places forming in you.*

February 2009

 Sally Allen McNall

The dawn raid

The usual strategy for millennia.

Hush. Sleep. Again.

Yesterday you did everything
you were supposed to, chatted,
danced, banked the fire.

Upturned, blind faces, mouths open,
limbs unfolded, in the skin tent,
a few centuries into your long journey
out of Africa.

Or you crowd into this lonesome day,
the many gods of your unfinished dreams
still trembling in you.

This is the time.

Out of the overshadowed sky,
the world forest, down
from the naked ridge
on scarcely broken horses.

Hush.
You would do it yourself.

Surprise. Pried open. Again.

You half-wake in your own place,
loss you have not begun to imagine
finding out your core.

Interpretation

This morning I dreamed myself
knee deep in a warm ocean of fresh blood.
Our dreams are free of us, and ruthless,
and even I cannot outtalk them, but
I can explain a few things. It was human.
It was not women's blood. It was not blood shed
in war—I know, I know, you didn't expect me
to say that just now, and it is a departure, but I'm
perfectly sure of it. It was not the blood of children
shot by other children, or—but this is going
nowhere. There are bloody deaths everywhere always.

There's something exciting about the color
of blood, so bright at first against any
human skin—like the flowers that attract
the hummingbird, the first color a baby tracks
when he is bored by black and white, the color
of celebration, of fuck-you cars and whorehouse lights,
color in flags, signals, color of fire, oh, it takes
the eye all right, it wakes you up.

As I woke up, heart speeding along
some nighttime freeway. In some
danger.

It's in the blood, they still say,
blood is pure, blood is mixed,
blood is a carrier of power, flaw, talent, trait,
long patience, insolence, easy rage.

Sally Allen McNall

I think my dream is meant to drop into you,
like each small soul back into that other,
wider ocean—to fall, dilute, yearn, join.

2003

The unfinished

Half blind Degas went back to his "experiments,"
as he called them, his "exercises"
in wire and wax.

"I'm just tired of everything," the old woman says,
"Brushing my teeth is too boring."

His dancers have no faces, no fingers, their limbs and bodies
elongate, broaden, truncate, dwindle. Slapped wax slabs
of arm, thigh, frozen in place like the old woman's hands.
Bronze dancers cast in knots, clumps, welts, flattened
fallings off from the original armature.

"Turn off that light," says the old woman. "It hurts my eyes,"
and "My eyes are fine," and "I'm resting my eyes," and "The print
is too small."

for MMA
2002

 Sally Allen McNall

Concrete particulars

For A

Yes, but in this book of horrors you refuse,
this documentation of systematic, categorical death,
writer and reader must step back, if only a step,
or tenderness could not touch the dead, as it must.

Remember the green eyes of the Afghani girl
on the magazine cover, at the beginning,
and how when they found her again,
well before the end, she was already old.
Remember the picture on the Internet?
We never saw her in the midst of life,
remember? So what do we have to go on
but the effort of thought in the unmapped darkness?

Harvest

As a child I was taken through Texas oil fields,
terrified of the heavy beaked drills, nodding, nodding.

I cried and cried.
I did not know how to put my questions.

When is a drought not a drought, what is a water mine?
What are trees for, what is an oil mine?

Later, off shore from scarred New Orleans
and at the North Sea a mile or two from Scotland's

Black Isle, I look away. What is dust?
What is not? What follows this? Where does it go?

2010

 Sally Allen McNall

In Scar

1.
One kind of a sentence is a scar
and of that kind
most kinds

(sentences left deep in the belly decades ago
all you knew then was you were often angry or sad)

most   are   now most

are "the politics of the latest atrocity"
            detonating in the kitchen
                        in the crowded street

keloid scars, habituated, impermeable

2.
One kind of not-sentence
            A_____, who is Jewish, hears as a bat hears
            a sentence about Israel   her escape   leaving a scar

as a non-sentence non-spoken to a F______   etc.

3.
Shields: wood, bone, hide, bronze, leather, mail, plates or scales,
polycarbonate Lexan® riot shield (available on eBay), eggshell,
womb, "bubble boy disease," fragmentation, Kevlar® blanket,
tattoo, rings

4.
Scab. Picking at the scab.

Bedsores. Ritualized display of the running bedsores.

Humans invented belief so that they would know whom not to believe.

November 2004

                                                                    Sally Allen McNall

From **_Studies in a Dead Language_**

The root of all evil

is the love of real estate, the boneless logic
that took the trees behind your house
a bare 150 years after the miners absorbed
the woods, spit out the valley tribes.

It's swallowed the six other sins whole,
so that even the very rich lie awake
dry-mouthed, plotting how to feed
anonymous habits: is it envy? sloth?

The rest get off on red meat and guns,
as if this were natural.

The droughts will make the rice go away
and then the wheat, faster than
the family farm went. Name
some virtues, I dare you.

What has Athens to do with Jerusalem?

In the open, busy marketplace,
questions, questions.

From a man who feared poets
the crazy idea
that nothing is real but only
copies of the real
which is elsewhere.

This is what the Hellenes
had to say to the Hebrews,
it is what Mohammed heard
on his journey through the night,

a curse still falling
through all our generations.

Sally Allen McNall

Seize the day

Coastal weather has moved inland.
It's as if I'd never left the ocean,
never returned to tall pines
waiting for dry storms and wildfires.

On a sunless day, the brutal headlands near the mouth
of the Russian River were gates, swung and fixed in place
against loud cold sea. The fort was built there anyway.

Trees upriver were here before Spain,
and the scarlet ice plant and lichen
against many-angled gray stones. Now they too
may be counted among our casualties.

The more reason to hold them, at least, in mind
next to this madrone, its wet trunk and branches
great arteries lifted out into the still air.

It cannot be said
into the eyes of another

One of those strangled wakings when the dream
however inconsequential feels heavy as death
and you throw it off you try to throw it off
blankets comforter the American Way
of Life the weight of a long dying, for
example your Father's dying over
years, the regress so slow, the
cane the walker the memory
loss the conservatorship
the incontinence the lost
ability to read the
refusal to get
out of bed

And you the good daughter or son
making light of it all smiles hugs
laughter even, paying extra to
make sure he is kept clean
paying extra to make
sure he is gotten
out of bed

It's the best I can come up with, I know
a nation is not a person, a nation is
—unlike a corporation—not even
legally a person and yet the
loneliness the squalid
details

                                        Sally Allen McNall

the accumulation of details, his licking
the plate, diarrhea, the peculiar
outfits, how you struggle
to overlook the
details

because if you make a picture of all
the details, but I don't do that here
I don't say it I don't look
into your eyes

2006

Dark Light

Going to the theatre

In Shakespeare's really bad play, the girl is raped,
her hands chopped off, her tongue cut out.

I've seen this done with long red ribbons
and with gauze and dribbling stage blood—

doesn't matter, it's Shakespeare, the whole
audience knows how she'll finally use

her stumps and a stick to spell in dirt the attacker's
name. *Uhn, uhn* she goes, and we don't hear,

air so rife with other language we can't think
of the loss of language, the loss of the way

our electrical brains pick out the craziest
little connections—wit, we call it. Or conspiracies.

Today, around the world, long streets fill
with the spoken word *peace*. An actor knows

that once the lips part from the initial sound,
the tongue flattens, pulls back, the lips stretch wide before

the final hiss, tongue pointed at teeth.
We leave the play, we dream real blood.

March 15, 2003
(War declared on Iraq March 19)

Dark light

Halo

Memory lights
its jewels
and its instruments
of torture with indiscriminate, small
flickering halos

to store them, you must be startled

you can't will yourself
into recollection
or its opposite

Stone

Before she knows how bad it is
her mind makes a space
encloses

peripheral detail:
broad hands, tile pattern, reek
noise she makes

as if she were lifting stone
into place on a wall
as she is

Sally Allen McNall

Fires

You were wondering night before last
did the Greeks and Trojans
all have PTSD so
it was ordinary as glory

or was it about weapons
a shield a shield
a sword a sword
an enemy a man

rather than
a bloody cloud
of sand or glass
lifting you
or them up away from the flame

The mind fires, fires, fires

Perfect

In the city we bought
cheese, a round of bread
two perfect peaches

we stopped to eat among the pines
we licked each other's fingers clean
so ripe those peaches
a thought could bruise them

Supply

She will never willingly
speak of the field hospitals

you must supply her
with your need to hear
about it

Edge

This morning you were wondering
if for the Trojan women
(raped, exiled, enslaved)
memory was ever consolation
retrieval of moments so soaked
in joy
they might ride the edge of the blade

Sally Allen McNall

Listening to Keats

If the math is beautiful, it is true.

Pay attention: the physicists
are describing the structure
of the universe.

In that bad London air
that stoked his disease, he staged
his raids on time-as-we-know-it.
From the grave he holds
his warm hand toward us, stops
his line there, two and a half
iambs in . . .

If the math is true, it is beautiful.

Pay attention: Keats tells you
how you can make a soul,
even—especially—
when there is no more true autumn,
even when the moving waters have given up
washing.
          Pay attention to
his roughened young Cockney voice
between shallow breaths. He is dying
a little bit at a time in Rome. For him,
death holds its appeal.

2008

Invoking Whitman

The prairie grass is green. June here is lilac season, and lilacs
fill two vases, so the house is full of perfume
which Whitman spoke against.

"Walt, I'm alone for the moment. I have some questions.
Do you know that it is no longer safe to allow the sea
to lick your naked body all over with its tongues?
That it is not clean forever and forever?

What do you make of that? Don't give me five iambs of death
for an answer."
He looks away, silent, like a man non-plussed, but
there's that willingness of his, and he turns back to say,
"What beautiful lilacs you have."

We talk then for a while about Lincoln, soldiers, Obama,
anxious love, New York, and the San Francisco Ferry,
which I recommend he ride on. He leaves the door open,
but undamaged, when he goes.

2009

 Sally Allen McNall

The back of the cave

Have you noticed that if you put something in a poem
your memory of it lights up, or theatrically darkens?
It's true. Once I say it in print it happened (even if
not exactly). I believe in it. Even before you read it,
all the details lock into my own system of what is really
important. I learned to love, for examples, all porcupines
in National Parks, Westerns filmed in Morocco, tea
in China. I have taken a private pride in the red high tops my
granddaughter wore once, and in an elephant at the Toledo zoo.
I will always grieve a lost shard of blue and white pottery.
This isn't to say I care less about other things, it's just,
connections are made. And maybe I know what she felt,
that elephant mom, or—in light of the pottery shard—how loss
is always somehow shared around. If I write you a poem
you know I love you. If I speak in your voice you
know I know you really well, and best when I've
finished writing. Does this work for oceans? For the moon?
I think you have the answer. I have a personal stake
in certain phases of the moon (see poems) and in the
Pacific (*passim*). History marches around in my work lately
like the loser army it is. I follow that army, whatever
that makes me, because it is instructive and takes my mind off
the future, like granite formations and luminescent lives
of the deep (see poems). We've had quite a ride.
What panache, what dubious, splendid trophies! If I
weren't always ready to pick up the pen, what could I say
we've stored at this point? No, I'd never say that.

In defense of lists

When you have begun a good list, it is difficult to stop.
In the *Iliad*, the armies muster as if for the first time—
the long lists of the warriors, the catalogue of ships. The war
is in its tenth year. The war must continue.
Whitman sings of every American he can imagine, for seven pages,
and travels the country over for nine pages more. It is still not,
no matter what he says, enough.

You see, it is not a matter of the time or the people,
who will hearten themselves in this manner in any age or land,
by the systole and diastole of alone and together.

It is what we do best, this keeping count of one another,
whatever our reasons. For this, we made ourselves over,
into the creatures who speak, boast, lie, count, record, promise
and list. Don't try to deny the impulse. Have you never,
on the edge of sleep, watched face after face glide
over the mind's dark lens, faces you could not imagine
in daylight, such is their infinity of strange detail?

How long have you remembered names and numbers of people,
Knowing you would not see them again? How often do you make
pointless lists, as if they mattered? Groceries, chores, weapons,
varieties of iris. Appointments, favorites, targets, what to pack.
Impossible losses. Some gains. Varieties of pain or pleasure.
Errands, charitable deductions, books, wars, birds.

One another. Don't stop. Count yourself in.

1999

                                                       Sally Allen McNall

Close

Like a twin you almost absorbed in the womb,
your misery kicks its little legs

out from your chest even when you are laughing
wildly or telling the latest hilarious tale of perfidy,

meanness, failure, pain, or of course your terrible
childhood. I want to take your misery by

its little damp heels and yank it out, a risky
breech delivery—or I want to amputate,

close as I would have to go
to your halfgrown heart.

A few hard words

for E and E

Once you lifted the baby up for her peace and yours, held her
to the long window's dark mirror where your shared misery
dissolved in its floating reflections: child, mother, wet
eyes amazed at each other, widening. That's over, forget it.
It is three a.m. in the city, she's fourteen, she's breaking your heart.

A mother likes to believe she can read a daughter's mind.
There's a long history behind this magic act—
signs, signals, vigils, closed envelopes, total recall.
The oracle's smoke twists up from the cave oily as ever,
as open to misinterpretation by the protagonist, who is not, now, you.

My friend the famous psychotherapist once said *You can be
anything you want to be.* But I said, and I say now *Bullshit.*
Billy Hume in junior high said he could swim the Atlantic
ocean if he wanted to. (A dumb kid destined, like the boy
in *Titanic,* to turn blue, but probably not for love.) So I

will not yell at you *Get a life.* But it is time for you to start
staying home from the shipwreck. And your girl, adrift
on her body's biochemical sea, seasick, and fixed on discovery?
She'll start to count lifeboats one of these years. Now, nothing
she hears keeps her back from her blood-logged, breathless

sheer drop deep down, thrumming with power. You remember
what a mirror is to a solitary girl, the drag and detail of it
like double gravity and half the electromagnetic spectrum, worlds
no one else sees. You know. For her peace, she wants you off
her dark screen. Your heart will be used against you.

                                                          Sally Allen McNall

Love and beauty

for S

are words a poet should use sparely if ever, and only if she can set them down
in the physical world, as in your voice on the phone, reliably filled with delight,
full of years of telling the almost untellable, of our long tumbles of talk.

Do you know someone's written software that recognizes image
after image of young, beautiful girls, supermodels, stars, morphing
the image toward the "ideal?" Perfectly pointless, if you ask me.

This article, in the <u>Scientific American</u>, does not mention
the controversy over what beauty is, scientifically speaking, *for.*
Evolutionary biologist say not for love, only for genetic replication,

and not even the seen, but rather the beholder's-- while neurology
and our present knowledge of the brain's electro-chemistry suggest
an infinity of provocations to love. It's not necessarily true,

then, that women our age might as well be invisible. And just now
in the parking lot I threw two sentences across my shoulder as did
Isadora her daring scarf, the death of her--and three women, a girl,

two men and two little boys turned from their own conversations,
sun in their eyes, shaken out of the middle of the day, dazzled,
to look, to see, who would love who forever, and why.

In the Rare Book Room

First you must show
you have a right
to go in.

Who you are.

You may carry nothing
but paper and a few
sharp pencils.

What you will give up.

Everything else
the librarian holds
while you work.

What you will risk.

The room is two-thirds
empty.

Who is with you.

The velvet page weights
are too heavy
for the small book
tied with worn ribbon
leather back
crumbling.

Who you hope to learn from.

You are as careful
as you can be.

Where you hope to go.
What you hope to save.

Sally Allen McNall

Six wooden blocks
for GDM

—named revenge, remorse
repentance, regret
remembrance, release

You might spend
a whole morning
stacking them
in one order
then another

You might work
chronologically
theologically
or attempt magic

Each is stained
a different color,
shades of indigo and violet
none pale

They are fashioned
of heartwood,
oiled, heavy,
never softening
to the touch

The iron thing they carried
I will not carry

—after Mary Oliver

I will carry it. For every child who cannot let it go. Notice
I do not mention compassion, that soft thing, with its shiny billowing.
Notice I do not even mention love, which seeds itself like a fat weed,
covers broken earth in one season, with and without reason.

Each winter I empty my closets of everything I have not worn for two years.
Books are harder to weed. I manage it.   But how can I give up
a single life that has contended with mine for pain or joy? They come with me,
shades, mistakes and miseries of my life, a long line of refugees, home.

I won't close the door behind me. When I have to flee over the rooftops
a crowd comes along, tumbling like the ninjas that souls must be,
making themselves (as Keats put it; I keep Keats) strong and beautiful.
So what if each holds some narrowing sickening secret?

So what if we don't get up to watch the sun rise, or surprise the wild geese
at their stopover on the high lake in the sierras? So what if we don't read
Emerson, or for that matter, don't read? I tell everyone *not to let it fall.*
I am not through with you, Mary. I lift for you part of the weight

you carry. Yes, you do.

                                                     Sally Allen McNall

Escape from the hospital

You have to suppose it happens a lot:
the skinny girl with bald patches where
she pulls out one hair at a time slides out
the front door, the old man finds
his smeared eyeglasses and coat
and takes the elevator to the parking lot.

In movies, all the time, someone does it
to escape a killer, or establish his basic
bare-ass silliness. Yet in real life
it begins with someone saying
Enough, whether or not others agree
with the decision. A mother picks up
her weeping boy, a man pulls the IV
from his wife's blackened arm, alarms
go off, the doctor is paged, the man
goes on batting the nurses off and detaching
the monitors, they make it down
the gleaming hall and the stairs—another
alarm going off—out into the hot morning,
to the car. There are of course consequences.

The most ordinary is death, what my friend
spoke of this morning as "a good death," maybe.
Lawyers may come into it. Psychiatrists.
The police. But none of this is the point:
we can't all be thinking *How complicated, how impossible,*
or we would all be lying flat somewhere enduring
the indignity and the fear that washes through us
during nights of rudely broken sleep and the unrelenting

company of strangers, we would all be citizens of nothing
with no plans and nowhere to go.

                                                    2008

                                    Sally Allen McNall

Writing to you from Dresden
—for Scott

Listen, if I couldn't do it any other way, I would tear a hole
in the world to get to you and not even worry about the blood
because bright and black blood is everywhere, as it has always been,
and here and there torn body parts, and different kinds of smoke.
Why would this message, just because it is personal,
come to you in private? I am in deepest green post-military
Europe and I smell it on every corner because
I have never smelled it, so nothing/everything hurts,
though not enough, and I don't know how to help it.

It's cold and raining here in July, the rain sluices the tiles, purls
and runs along the gutters, goes back into the ground like blood,
like water and blood did while would be emperors hacked their way
into whole populations, doing what is in all of us to do

just like rain down a rainspout, rain pouring everywhere,
and then not. Like after a flood. Like fresh water gone
suddenly missing under asphalt everywhere. I miss you
so much I am writing this, imagining because we are
well known to each other, we are well known to each other.

                                                    July, 2009

Time Spent Waiting

River, mountain

1.

The brown river, swift, steady,
a little higher each day and then not
and then slowing,

the mountain behind it
bare on one slope, where rock faces
oppose wind carrying away from the fire
visible and invisible detritus,
the great trembling net of everything
torn and dry, the mountain
snowy with ash,

the brown river dry, its bed exposed,
round rocks dusted with

the evidence.

2.

We did our best to understand.
We walked upright
to this.

The sun's pulse, timed,
burning gong calling now now now
to us, in our cage of air.

2008

TIME SPENT WAITING

Knowing, not knowing, 1

Like a woman heavily pregnant

                the child hasn't moved

these six days

this is in another century, or country so

                nothing to be done
                wait and see

Like a sign: FALLING ROCKS

you keep on pedaling

           don't you

Afterward

Among those untouched by the flames
some said to themselves

let it go

and they remember the weird light-headed moment
the yearning

Sally Allen McNall

Knowing, not knowing, 2

Why these outsize brains?
Lobes lopping over simple want or contentment
Neurons untwining

                imagining, moving into

prayers   cities   octaves   the laboratory

Awareness of time to plan

                or not

Big-brained, helpless
      we lull each laden synapse
              binding us to the living world

Plus or minus

It's like a weak electrical charge, this fear, it can wear you out
but set you going, too—impossible, a whole day
without plugging into it somehow, as if there were some timer to which
we are all connected

Knowledge

it arrives dragging all its tribe and its boundaries and treaties
or it doesn't arrive

remember high school history, the boring boring industrial revolution?

in Chemistry, carbon dioxide
in Geography, imports and exports
in French, the subjunctive and pluperfect
and so on through all the books

a glimpse of a part of time, a luminescent edging, a balancing form of words,
we made our way here as if on stepping stones in our common rivers
that today threaten levees banks irrigation systems reservoirs

threaten to leave, or course in new ways, obliterating and suspending
the topsoil in which our maps were planted

Sally Allen McNall

Cease your struggle

Be a sailing ship creaking away with a cargo of bones.
Be a river, or a bright sheet of water falling.
Be the yellow leaves of the sycamore in the big storm.

Lose the right engine, then the left engine.
Be the torn air.
Be an animal that has learned to fear us.

Be the martyr translated to pink mist.
Be the hands carrying food, or carrying garbage.
Be snow beneath sun, or the climber who hears the avalanche begin.

Watch a child die of hunger.
Go onstage howling and high.
Collect enough debris and ice to reflect light. Then orbit.

Be the mountain mudhouse in the earthquake.
Descend the fallopian tube.
Be the forest canopy as it ignites.

Come home

so much talk now
about saving the
other creatures

the birds we've forever
used for our souls
in prayer and poem

for any human wish
because they fly
because they return

what of a soul
that scurries across
the kitchen floor

or breaks its heart running
around a man-made circle
a man on its back

or hangs one-armed, swinging
from one polished branch
glassed-in

or leaves the air
to sing long philosophies
in the roiled deep

Sally Allen McNall

Is a human soul quick, can it
turn coat, change shape, carry
a weapon, see the edge

does it shrivel like a cast
snakeskin or is it
the bright-armored snake

is it a handful of seeds cast
in the moist dark, a corm curled
in on its pattern

can we now
let it go
let it return home

Clear night

Stars

How surprised we were
when we heard
that some starlight

came so far to us
it left itself behind
going out

Most of us
looking up
don't remember
to think

> here and there
> no stars
> only light

Sun, moon

A moon so bright you could
read print by it

> silly as that

would be

> Oh moon

> you have

been all the things
people could imagine

Sally Allen McNall

The sun rushes toward us
like death

you alone watch with us

All day in the open

exposed

                    city intersections, highways
each car and corner a violent emptiness

(people will travel hundreds of miles)

only yesterday a journalist got out of the helicopter
walked around on the new Arctic breakaway ice sheet

amazing feeling
he said

                                        2007

Sally Allen McNall

Shelter

The house has eight rooms, or more. You try
to measure it against the long history
of useful human dwellings, or

to measure it against all the tent cities and camps
of the present, still there, though at first
we called them temporary.

You try, you fail, moving from room to room as if
these were gestures of the soul, as if the soul
needed all this geography.

Maybe it does, maybe it forgets easily and needs
wide windows that look out on trees, or needs
curtains, to remind it how

to stay aloof from its own suffering, held, walked
like a newborn, back and forth to rest.
Lost to the world

which will find you. This moment it seeks you out.

Last at the feast

Six lost peacocks come to the courtyard, mornings—sun on the deck, play tag, or at least run in circles in the bushes, stop to preen like embarrassed cats, chase juncos and chickadees from scattered seeds.

My mind runs right off into history again—a cave-like medieval kitchen where over a great fire an entire ostentation of peacocks roasts on spits, and then is served as the entremet, plumage gilded and put back in place. Or of course the deporable Romans, sprawled on their comfy lecti, nibbling peacocks' tongues.

Sometimes I see wild turkeys here, Ben Franklin's pick for National Bird. When fifty-six men signed the land up for freedom, for dinner they could've had Maryland crab cakes, oysters, smoked fish or pork, venison, salads from summer vegetable gardens, plenty of fine ale, the best ice cream in the Thirteen.

Remember our allies, the French? Ben enjoyed the Court so much; Tom, less. Petit fours were just in, puff pastry, foie gras, chocolate, coffee. Dozens of candles lit in every room, the king ate enough for three, Marie entered with a ship full sail on her head,
never said a word about people and cake.

This Thanksgiving I paid triple for a turkey bred the old fashioned agile way, lived a happy turkey life. Who am I kidding?—this is food extreme as Versailles' or Rome's.

Those signers—they didn't imagine abundance would be so brief. I barely glimpse the boundlessness they saw. How giddy they were, and why not?

And here the silly lost peacocks, for no reason, all fan their tails.

2010

                                          Sally Allen McNall

"Fallings from us, vanishings"

—Wordsworth, Ode, *Intimations of Immortality*

You say goodbye to your unhappy childhood,
yet for years you turned to the sad mother, the angry father,
for love—not to plants, birds, sunrise nor the words of the prophets
of the soul in all things. For years your soul tarried,
because it was, like so many, a good, hopeful soul
and tried to find a straight way where crooked pain was.
Do you think you learned nothing, those years?
You learned how to love. And I say, forget
that it turned to fear and finally indifference, forget
that hope had to be relearned later and elsewhere, forget
your thousand poems to the members of other species.

In that first nest, first dark burrowing, you learned
to love because you had to, to survive. You knew this, then.
Now there are other questions of survival before you.
There is anger everywhere in the world and sorrow
following. Even the Buddha would not tell you to forget
this, while you are busy remembering the bobolink,
snow-cricket, brown bat, peony, honeysuckle.

The End of Lists

Homer started it, with his long sun-varnished catalogue of ships
and arms,
all the arts of war.
Whitman put in the foam of everything large and small, stars,
weeds, us,
the wholeness of the world.
End-stopped lines stretching like latitudes
over page after page.

War still scrolls its names
on a dark screen.

Oh, but it was sweet a while,
the naming of all wonders, as if
they were inexhaustible.

December 2008

 Sally Allen McNall

Nothing Lost

Nothing lost

—for SE

1. Artesian Aquifer

countless years in the dark   under rock under pressure
this water flies toward the sky   a glass tower turning
outward in dispersal   droplets finer and more fine
soft on your lifted face   nothing lost of the overflow
as it soaks to join the groundwater   also recharged by rain

2. The Great Saray of Istanbul

the water that once charged this cistern   arrived by aqueduct
under Aya Sofya under Justinian and from somewhere else
came reused marble   two Medusas assembled
one head upside down   the other tilted away
beneath the basilica   in silent chanting dark

3. So Deep My Love

you cannot quite follow the words   nor I the music
in trust we listen as the water leaps up   gallops, falls
into the last dry corner   of each oddly assembled heart

February 2008

Yosemite, October

Altitude

your heart beats in your ears
your breath thins, coarsens

there is nothing between
your skin and the sun

who came so far?

Waterfall

early morning shadow
of canyon wall

move through it
cautiously, as if to
an oracle

water sifts downward

above, in new sunlight
a line of water on fire

Meadow, afternoon

all the grass
gone golden

Sally Allen McNall

a meander
icing over
turns and turns

short grass and stones
glint underfoot

don't move

Granite by moonlight

full moon
harvest moon

tall rooted rockface
a third
of what the spectrograph shows

across its ivory a thick stroke of dark
from a Zen brush

behind it stars
in sky become delicate
as midnight tissue paper

The burn

because you have seen its like
now, more than once

it can be let go
like the oaks
gone variously golden

dogwood scarlet

fir   pine   hemlock
a handful of species
laurel   spruce

let go

Range

The Mesozoic is yesterday
here at the western terminus of the Modern

you can see

with care, you can flatten all you know
before this evidence

Road out

the rocks are uninterested
in the roads
and fall on them
when they can

2009

   Sally Allen McNall

Extending a metaphor

You want to keep an eye
on who you are

so when it's time you know
what can be tossed

overboard and what
to hang onto till you can't

anymore, don't be one of those
who can't tie down the soul and let it

roll back and forth on the deck
until it's breached and empty.

Drop the anchor of your darkness
down into the larger dark because

it's yours, you made it, you know how
how to keep it safe, below deck; secure

what you love, close to you
so you can take it out often

and make it shapely in a new
way, as you hoist it back into light.

Trying to close the distance

1.

on the walls of the hotel in Ourzazate,
movie posters of decades

in the lobby,
four Egyptian gods six feet tall

and a throne
from *Cleopatra*

tourists may use it
for photos

2.

movies once went to LA
for pure dry light

we stayed an extra day here between
holy Fes and the Sahara

this desert has not bloomed
easy to get men as extras, or crew

we walked back from dinner
under a round white moon

                    Sally Allen McNall

3.

in the morning
from a high wall on a hill
we looked down upon a woman in blue

in a high walled courtyard, her black goat,
her black rabbit

she hung clothes to dry
tethered the goat

you bent over the parapet
widened your lens

Lens

1.
To you I gave myself first in the body
and then in the mind, and later in the spirit.
I don't know if this is an ordinary course
of love. I don't know if it is true.
Yet I have been drawn along by our differences
as if by a new atlas, museum, trail sign.
Was I born a lover of compendia,
of the infinite responsiveness of the world's body,
or did I learn it, learning you?

2.
There is always a time when one of us says
"Get out the dictionary," and one of us does.
I have done so in the middle of the night,
adoring its heaviness, its silk-thin pages,
its tiny variations of typeface, its histories
of usefulness. How it has, like the body's heat
and unendurable suspense, its own
magnifying glass. This lens we tilt,
just so, over tinder. This roof of glass
through which we fall, in the sound of breaking,
into row on row of leaf, bloom, mist, darkened earth,
into all that packed, overlapping sweetness.

                                              Sally Allen McNall

3.
Each time we have changed houses there has been
another thirty cartons of books stacked
against the far wall of the double-load.
There's almost nothing, between the two of us,
that we haven't looked up, or don't intend to--
we've a drawer just for bookmarks,
in case we can't wait to read in sequence.
Our talk, walking in the morning, or late, on
the beach, or over dinner, in the presence of anyone,
is annotation, memo, prayer, promise and cautionary tale.
We have brought each other up
on decipherments and decryptions,
as if we two kept up, together, a ledger
as workable as Saint Peter's. Today's page,
tomorrow's. They mount up, there is always
one more for our quick overtake, new nomenclature,
general apologia, theory of everything, revision, revision--
Or as if we two owned a state-of-the-art instrument,
like the two Keck telescopes of Mauna Kea,
each light bucket separately moveable,
floating on oil bearings, in air quite still
below the trade winds--as we draw down
sun after distant sun, by the steadfast path of light, into our bodies.

4.
Where is the spirit but where the body
and mind conjoin, our comprehension
of that insatiable wholeness? If spirit is not
the deep peace brought by the other's touch,
the other's laughter, what could it be?
I could find a microscopic Eros is at work nearly everywhere
in this particular kitchen, this various garden,
and he is a god. Please hold the ladder once again
while I reach for something I want
for you, the weight not yet in my fingers.
Its ripeness will let it go easily into my hand.

                                                           Sally Allen McNall

NOTES

"WHAT IS BENEATH OUR FEET" The bridge over the Neretva River in Mostar, Bosnia, was a 500 year old structure integrated into buildings on either side. It was destroyed in the war by the Croats and is now rebuilt. The abbey of Belle Pais was established by Crusaders, In the sixties Turkish and Greek Cypriots lived and worked together in one country, although there was a Turkish quarter in Lefkosia, now the only divided city in the West.

"Dark Light" The color seen by the eye in perfect darkness

NOTES

"WHAT IS BENEATH OUR FEET" The bridge over the Neretva River in Mostar, Bosnia, was a 500 year old structure integrated into buildings on either side. It was destroyed in the war by the Croats and is now rebuilt. The abbey of Belle Pais was established by Crusaders, In the sixties Turkish and Greek Cypriots lived and worked together in one country, although there was a Turkish quarter in Lefkosia, now the only divided city in the West.

"Dark Light" The color seen by the eye in perfect darkness